"Diana's account is simple and powerful in its compassionate and promising message to bereaved parents. As a survivor of her own son's death, Diana is a wise companion and a courageous guide for others facing the daunting journey of the minefield called grief. She offers concrete, no nonsense description of the emotional, behavioral and physical fall-out faced by bereaved parents and offers heartfelt and meaningful reminders for self-care in spite of incomparable pain. Most importantly she shines a beacon of light on this new, albeit unwelcome new normal, encouraging the bereaved to find purpose and meaning as they slowly and tentatively face each tomorrow, while always maintaining the connection with our loved ones. Diana's deep respect and faith for other bereaved parents is the music behind every word written."

~ Marianne Esolen, L.M.S.W.
Grief Counselor and Consultant

"*Am I Going Crazy?* is a must read for all bereaved parents. There are many helpful suggestions on how to persevere one day at a time. I've come to realize that grieving for my beloved Christopher is a life-long arduous journey. Diana is a shining star. Her books do so much good in the world. In Mark Anthony's memory, Diana exudes a sense of peace and hope."

~ Kathy Montoya, Bereaved Mom

"As a bereaved sibling there are feelings that Diana clearly states during our grief process is normal. *Am I Going Crazy?* validates that I am not going crazy. The book helps me realize more things that my Mom is going through during her grief journey. We are now in our fourth year going down this different path after the loss of my brother Jason Lee and father Anthony."

~ Laura Ameruso, Bereaved Sibling

"As parents who lost their only son and a sister who lost her only sibling, we feel this book is a must read. This book provides a helping hand and great support for those who have lost their loved one. Although all emotions, feelings, and situations are unique for each individual, the book gently assists you through the journey of the grieving process."

~ Helene & Tim Horodnicki,
Bereaved Parents and Heather, Bereaved Sibling

"Ms. Roscigno's work on grief has been a gift for those coping with tremendous loss. In her recent work, *Am I Going Crazy?* she approaches the subject with incredible ease for the reader. Most especially this book helps the very newly bereaved or those who have not allowed themselves to deal with their feelings yet. When your loss is new and you are in sort of 'shock' mode, this book is something most people could actually absorb and benefit greatly from. Having lost my only son and my Dad within three months of each other, I can relate to every emotion, every feeling, and every question she poses in this book. YES! You often feel as if you are going crazy, but you are not. It is the territory of the trauma of loss. This book makes you feel normal, despite what society, friends, family, co-workers may expect of you in terms of 'getting on with it'. Grief is sneaky, cunning thing, in that it comes at you out of nowhere sometimes in odd ways that you are not expecting. I will be adding this book to our recommended list on GRASP, Grief Recovery After Substance Passing with no reservations. Thank you, Ms. Roscigno for yet another look into the process of grieving."

~Denise Angela Cullen, MSW, LCSW,
Certified Grief Recovery Specialist

"In *Am I Going Crazy?* Diana does a wonderful job of validating and normalizing the grief journey for bereaved parents. Her passion, honesty and commitment to service to others also are evident in her writing."

~ David Roberts, Bereaved Father,
Author of *Mourning Discoveries During the Holidays*

"Diana Roscigno speaks from the heart and soul. Her story is so inviting because we all find ourselves somewhere in that journey. Read the book. Share the book. Find a point of connection. 'Until we meet again…' is her dedicatory statement to Mark. We don't know when "until" is, but I know that Diana and Mark will always be parent and son and will always be in contact."

~Richard B. Gilbert, PhD, CT, Bereaved Parent,
Educator, Spiritual Caregiver, Speaker and Author who counts it a privilege to have met Mark through his Mom's stories, writings and feelings."

"Having lost your own child it is an inspiration to all of those whose life must go on without the ones they love. That is the whole point of this book you can survive this, you can go on and live. Truly have a life again and in doing so take every memory of your loved one with you. I will never forget someone telling me after the tragic loss of my nephew Sabby that I must now be his voice and to not only speak for him but to sing. I thought they were crazy at the time but now I realize you must go on for if my voice is silenced then so is Sabby's. I thank you again for your strength and for lighting the path for us to follow out of the darkness we now live. May God bless you and your son and every heart you touch with these words."

~ Cathy Crecco, Bereaved Aunt.

"Diana's book will resonate with, all bereaved parents, grandparents, siblings, family and friends. Diana has incorporated the emotions that we must endure from our severe pain. *Am I going Crazy?* has emotions and thoughts both silent and vocal that all grieving parents and siblings are feeling. We belong to a club that no one should ever belong to. Diana's journey through the pain of grieving has brought us to an understanding of what we all share. We will be grieving at different levels forever. No!!! We are 'Not' Going Crazy."

~ Mary Ameruso, Bereaved Mother

AM
I
GOING
CRAZY?

For bereaved parents, family members, friends, therapists and grief-related organizations

Diana M. Cimador Roscigno

By Diana M. Cimador Roscigno

Author of *I Am Still His Mother*
and *Grief: Is This Normal?*

Copyright © 2010 by Diana M. Cimador Roscigno

ISBN 0-7414-6395-4

Printed in the United States of America

Published May 2011

INFINITY PUBLISHING
1094 New DeHaven Street, Suite 100
West Conshohocken, PA 19428-2713
Toll-free (877) BUY BOOK
Local Phone (610) 941-9999
Fax (610) 941-9959
Info@buybooksontheweb.com
www.buybooksontheweb.com

DEDICATION

Mark Anthony Governale
June 20, 1985 – January 1, 2003

"Until we meet again my son
May you soar the Heavens
On angels' wings"

And

In honor of all children who have died too soon

MARK ANTHONY

Mark, or Markie as he was known, was the youngest of my three sons.

He was seventeen and a half when he was killed in a car accident on January 1, 2003. Against better judgment he went out that night, a decision that would cost him his life.
We don't know what caused his accident. There were no witnesses and no other car involved. He was the driver and only occupant of the vehicle.
What we do know is that he lost control, went airborne, landed upside down, snapped two trees, was partially ejected and killed on impact.

There is no question that my son's death has become part of my existence. I have no doubt that his death will be with me for the rest of my life, however so will his life.

Mark was a handsome, intelligent, sensitive, extraordinary young man with an incredible zest for life.

He was an awesome kid, kind, gentile, compassionate, unselfish, bright, energetic, accident prone, inquisitive and smart. He'd be the first to lend a helping hand, was known as the peacemaker, "go to guy" and occasional practical joker. He was outgoing and had an entertaining sense of humor.

He was the overachiever of our family, had been an honor roll student and excelled in everything he did.
He played tuba in the school band and was on the football and golf teams in high school.
There was no doubt in my mind that his intelligence, ambition, drives and accomplishments would have taken him far.

Outside of school activities included scouting, shooting hoops in the yard, playing baseball or softball, hitting balls at the golf driving range, photography, politics, hunting, target tournaments, white water rafting, and his job. Mark had won numerous target competitions with his bow and gun.

Mark had auburn red hair, brown eyes and a dimpled smile.
His favorite color was blue.
His favorite stuffed animal was Stimpy.
His favorite foods included fried chicken cutlets, seafood and venison.

His favorite candy bars were Twix and Kit Kat and favorite snacks were sunflower seeds or beef jerky.

Mark loved to read and often joined the library's summer reading club. His favorite book was *Call of the Wild*.

Halloween costume favorites were Dracula, Werewolf and Einstein.

His favorite television shows were The X Files, The Simpson's, South Park, PBS, History and Discovery channels.

Mark started playing sports on leagues when he was five years old.

At ten he announced he was going to be a wildlife conservationist when he grew up, and that wolves would be his specialty.

Hobbies included collecting; coins, baseball, dungeon and dragon cards, National Geographic magazines, coffee mugs, wildlife sculptures, paintings, posters and books.

Boating and fishing were summer pastimes as were vacationing in Myrtle Beach, Florida, Texas and St. Martin. He spent endless hours challenging the surf with his boogey board and combing beaches with his metal detector looking for buried treasures.

Mark was a hard worker and even shoveled snow for two winters to earn enough money to buy his first boat, a fourteen-foot aluminum rowboat.

At sixteen, Mark stood six foot three inches, weighed one hundred and sixty five pounds, had six pack abs and had reached a turning point in his life. I began to notice a change at home, with his schoolwork, sports, his job and himself. The Mark I knew was becoming a stranger to me.
At the close of tenth grade he announced he was going to go live with his father. I was a who, what, where, when Mom and he wanted his freedom. Mark never did move back home. The last time we saw each other was four months before he was killed.

Mark touched all who knew him in some way. He really was special and continues to make a difference in the world. Truly he is my light, my inspiration and the wind beneath my wings.

About the Author

I am a wife, mother, nurse and a bereaved Mom who has experienced the unimaginable heartbreak and insurmountable despair following the death of my son, Mark Anthony. His death redefined my life.
I didn't think I could or would survive and yet here it is almost eight years later and I have not only survived, I have reinvested in living life again.

Divorce, remarriage and other family dynamics have had a profound impact on my grief journey.

My journey began the morning of January 1, 2003 when I heard the words no parent wants to hear, "There's been an accident."

Never had I experienced such intense excruciating heartache. I wailed liked a wounded animal.
The void in my head, heart and soul were unbearable.
I wanted someone to tell me there had been a mistake.

All I wanted was my son.
I wasn't supposed to bury my child.

The estrangement between my son and me at the time of his death left me with an enormous sense of guilt that I had in some way contributed to his death. If I didn't let him go and live with his father, he'd be alive today. I shouldn't have let him go. He should have been home.

Emotionally I felt battered and beaten. Grief had consumed me.

I felt alone, lost, helpless, hopeless and afraid.

The simplest things depleted any energy I had and I barely functioned on autopilot.

I thought I was going crazy.

I wanted to escape but couldn't. My grief was with me when I went to sleep, when I awoke, in every tear I cried and breath I took.
I wanted someone to tell me how I was supposed to feel and if what I was feeling was normal.
I never thought I'd ever smile again or laugh.

Two years into my journey I reached a turning point.

Each of us makes choices that will determine how we process our loss and our grief journey. I made a choice to not let pain be the center of my world.

My grief journey has been nurtured through acceptance; hope for healing, survivorship and by working it everyday.

The bottom line is that I found what worked for me and went with it.
I have been an active member of The Compassionate Friends of Rockville Centre, New York since 2003.
By 2005 I started facilitating a death of a child support group at my local church. Giving back to others as others had given to me.
In 2007 I founded The Bereaved Parents of the USA Long Island, New York Chapter.
I wrote and published my first book, *I Am Still His Mother.*
In 2008 I wrote and published, *Grief: Is This Normal?*
I was the Chairperson of the 2009 Annual National Bereaved Parents of the USA Gathering Committee.
In 2010 I wrote, *Am I Going Crazy?*
I also founded the Long Island Chapter of Grief Recovery After Substance Passing a.k.a. GRASP.

I present workshops on both a regional and national level and welcome invitations to educate bereaved parents and those who interact with bereaved parents.

I am proof that survival is possible.

Not only can you survive you can thrive and honor your child's life by living yours.

To contact author

Diana M. Cimador Roscigno
PO Box 94 Bayville, New York 11709-0094
516-233-4848 or EM:
markanthonysmom@yahoo.com

ACKNOWLEDGMENTS

To my husband, Paul, who has been so patient and supportive of my endeavors as I continue to reach out to bereaved families.

To my children, grandchildren and family who have taught me that the greatest discovery and journey is within ourselves.

Jason Lee's sister, Laura Ameruso
Bereaved Sibling
Thank you for sharing and
contributing to this book
Dealing with a Bereaved Sibling

Jason Lee's mom, Mary Ameruso
Bereaved Parent

Kelly's dad, Mitch Carmody
Bereaved Father & Author of *Letters to My Son*

Sabby's aunt, Cathy Crecco
Bereaved Aunt

Jeffrey's mom, Denise Angela Cullen
Bereaved Parent and Director of GRASP
Grief Recovery After Substance Passing

Marianne Esolen, L.M.S.W.
Grief Counselor and Consultant

Rev. Richard Gilbert, PhD, CT

Ryan's mom and dad, Helene & Tim Horodnicki
Bereaved Parents

Ryan's sister, Heather Horodnicki
Bereaved Sibling

Christopher Eisele's mom, Kathy Montoya
Bereaved Parent

Jeannine Marie's dad, David Roberts
Bereaved Parent & Author of
Mourning Discoveries

Drew and Jeremiah's mom, Rosemary Smith
Bereaved Parent & Author of *Children of the
Dome* and the documentary film,
Space Between Breaths

The Compassionate Friends of
Rockville Centre, New York
Elaine & Joe Stillwell Chapter Leaders

CONTENTS

INTRODUCTION

To the bereaved reading this, I extend my heartfelt sympathy and hand in friendship.

For those helping others following the death of a child this book provides insight into the journey of parental and sibling grief.

I hope you will find this book to be a catalyst for change.
This guidebook/workbook doesn't just tell you that you can survive it tells you how to survive.
May it lead you from the depths of despair to hope, healing and survivorship.

It validates many of the common grief reactions bereaved families experience, Physically, Behaviorally, Emotionally and Spiritually, that you are not going crazy, and it offers information, with coping tools and skills for bereaved parents, family members, friends, therapists and grief related organizations.

"Although the world is also full of suffering,
It is also full of overcoming it"
Helen Keller

YOU ARE NOT GOING CRAZY

Grief is our natural way of responding to our loss.

The grief of a bereaved parent is unfathomable, incomprehensible and life altering.

What you feel as you grieve can be confusing. You may feel alone, lost, helpless, hopeless, bombarded, overwhelmed and bewildered by what you never thought was possible.

Parents are not supposed to bury their children.

You are entitled to ask yourself if what you are feeling is normal or abnormal.

Someone you love has died and you are hurting.

You are grieving and mourning the death of a child.

It is not without pain and suffering.

This is not something you "get over".

You will never get over the death of your child, however you can get through it.

You will be challenged to discover who you are now that your child has died.

A bereaved parent is always the parent of the child who has died.

Feeling as if you are going crazy or falling apart at the seams is part of your grief process.

This is a journey that is endured, processed and expressed through our emotions, feelings, thoughts, reactions and responses, which are natural, necessary and within your "New Normal".

HOW COULD THIS HAVE HAPPENED?

There must be a mistake.
A parent is not supposed to bury their child.
It just isn't natural.

All I want is my child.
I just want my child.
What do I do now?
What am I supposed to do?
Someone please wake me up from this
nightmare.

Am I going crazy?

Why did this happen?
Why did God let this happen?
It isn't right.
It isn't fair.
Why didn't God take me instead of my child?

Where is my child now?
Is my child in pain or suffering?
Will I ever see my child again?
Can my child see me?
Am I going to forget my child's face, smile,
voice, smell or touch?

Am I going crazy?

Who am I now that my child is dead?
Am I still my child's mother or father?

What do I say when someone asks how many children I have?
Did I fail as a parent?
Will I survive?
Will my family survive?
I want someone to tell me how I am supposed to do this.

How long am I going to feel like this?
I take one step forward and slide back two.
Will I ever smile again?
How can I be happy when my child is dead?
How can I partake in festive occasions?
I just want things to go back to the way they were.
The harsh reality is that you can't go back to the security and comfort of what once was.

Am I going crazy?

I expect my spouse to know what I need and when I need it, but what I really want is my child back.
I just want to die and to be with my child.

Everyday is a challenge to feel alive when your world is crumbling and nothing is as it once was.

I have no drive, ambition or purpose.
It is an effort to get out of bed when you have little or no energy at all.
The simplest things of everyday life become unimportant, frivolous, insignificant and non-essential.

I don't care if the sink is full of dishes.
I don't care if the laundry basket is overflowing.
I don't care if the bills get paid on time.
Nothing matters.
I just don't care anymore.
Life has no meaning.

Am I going crazy?

I walk around in a fog-like state of mind.
I travel to and arrive at my destination with no recall of the trip there.
I forget the day of the week, to keep appointments and what I went to the refrigerator for.

How can life go on around me as if nothing has happened?
What's wrong with people don't they realize my child has died?
Frustrations mount when my expectations of people are not met.

Am I going crazy?

People avoid me as if I have a plague, ducking and dodging me as if the death of my child is contagious.
They look and act differently around and toward me, change the subject when I mention my child's name and there are awkward moments of silence.
Some even make insensitive remarks.
Why do they do that?
Don't they realize how painful that is for me?
Hearing my child's name lets me know that my child is remembered.
I don't want my child forgotten or erased.

Am I going crazy?

I need to feel connected to my child.
I search for signs from my child.
I smell my child's clothes and pillow.
I wrap myself up in my child's blanket and lay on my child's bed.
My child's room has become a shrine.

Am I going crazy?

Sometimes I catch myself looking at another child and wonder if their life will be cut short.

There are times when I can cry for hours or not shed a tear.

Grief burst come when you least expect them most, even if you try to resist them and they stay for as long as they need to.

They happen at the bank, in the car, shower, doctors office, the supermarket, restaurants, basically anywhere they want.

I yearn for and miss my child beyond words.

Am I going crazy?

AM I SUPPOSED TO FEEL LIKE THIS?

There are many factors and variables that influence and impact a bereaved parent's grief journey.

They can include:

How your child died (sudden death, prolonged illness, miscarriage, stillborn, murder or suicide)

How you were told and by whom

The child's birth order and sex (for bereaved parents the age of the child that has died has no relevance)

The wake, funeral services or rituals

Your personality

Your age (influences your ability to understand death and dying)

Your relationship with your child

Your health

Past deaths

Unresolved loss

Myths

Life's stressors regarding (home, family, career, finances, religion, spiritual and cultural beliefs)

The change of seasons

Weather

The time of day

These are just some of the factors and variables that can create differences in your grief process.

Your grief is as individual as you are and the circumstances surrounding your child's death.

By allowing yourself to feel and experience grief's most intense heart wrenching pain you can move toward a life in which pain is not the center of your world.

Even though each of our journeys is an individual one, we share many of the same common grief reactions and changes, which are natural, necessary and normal.

Physically

A hollow empty void in the pit of your gut or a lump in your throat

Fatigue and exhaustion are constant companions

Your grief will consume more energy than you would have imagined

It is an effort to get out of bed, dress, brush your teeth or hair, answer the phone, engage in conversation, eat, drink, run a household, work and remember to breathe

Sighing

Heartache

A heaviness or tightness in your chest, racing of your heart or palpitations

Shortness of breath

Sleep disturbances; trouble falling asleep, staying asleep, dreams, nightmares, flashbacks or grinding of teeth during sleep

Digestive changes, nausea, vomiting or stomach ache

Appetite changes, loss of appetite, not eating or binge eating comfort food

Weight fluctuations, loss or gain

Dehydration, dry mouth, lips, eyes or skin

Speech patterns change, often lose your thought midstream of a sentence

Feel weak, dizzy, unsteady gait

Hypersensitive to surroundings or startle easily

Experience a change in sex drive

Headaches, migraines

Muscle aches, twitches

Chronic aches and pains

Compromised immune system and increase in illnesses

Behaviorally/Emotionally

Shock and numbness undeniably shield you from what your mind simply rejects

Go through the motions

Have no drive or ambition to do anything

Nothing really matters anymore

Diminished self-care, content to stay in pajamas for days; lament on the couch or in bed

Become overactive (workaholic, cleanaholic, or shopaholic)

Binge shopping may result in excessive debt and doesn't fill the void

Less productive

Inability to concentrate for periods of time

Difficulty focusing, reading or balancing a checkbook

Feel scattered and be easily distracted

Experience memory loss like appointments, the time, day, month, and year, to pay bills or lose things

Leave the house with different colored socks or shoes on, put clothes on inside out

Poor decision-making and problem solving at home or in the workplace, grief does not allow you to think clearly

Day to day task seem frivolous and non-essential

Shopping, cooking and housework are not high on the priority list

Depression

A need to tell and retell your story

Crying or not shed a tear, sobbing, weeping

Hold onto linking objects and look for signs (pennies from heaven, birds, rainbows, butterflies, dragonflies, feathers, dreams)

Preserve keepsakes

Post Traumatic Stress Disorder

Isolate, withdraw or become antisocial, family gatherings remind us that our child is not present and that circumstances have changed

Address books and emails change

Avoid situations that arouse grief

Overprotective of loved ones, fear of losing them

Mood swings

Agitation and lashing out irrationally

Anger is a very real part of the grief process

It reminds us that we are alive

It can be directed at anytime to self, spouse, significant other, deceased child, immediate family members, extended family, friends, employers, coworkers, healthcare providers, emergency response teams, law enforcement, clergy, congregation or even strangers

Anger is hurtful to you as well as others

Suppressed it can lead to feelings of isolation, betrayal, desertion and nightmares

It consumes energy and time, compromises your health and prevents resolution of your grief

The best plan of action is to let it out

Guilt, real or imagined, is a normal part of a grief journey

It is toxic, postpones, limits, delays and diverts the grief process

It is natural to think that you could have done something to prevent the death of your child

If only _____

I should have _____

What if _____

Nothing evokes guilt like the death of a child

There are always regrets for things said, unsaid, done and undone

Bad times overshadow the good times

Reduce self-punishment; you did the best you could

Guilt has a way of haunting, misleading and manipulating us

Ask yourself if the guilt you are experiencing is based on misdeeds or wrongful intent?

Spiritually

Feel abandoned by church, clergy or congregation

Question beliefs and faith

Am I being punished?

Is there eternal life?

Will I see my child again?

Can my child see me?

Is my child in pain or suffering?

Is my child at peace?

Feel anger toward God or turn to God and prayer

Sense child's presence

Uncharacteristic religious involvements (psychics/mediums)

Search for meaning or purpose in life

SELF REFLECTION EXERCISE

The following is a list of words that you may or may not identify with.

Find the words that best describe you and reflect how you have felt or are feeling.

Circle the words, jot them down on a separate piece of paper or write in the space provided.

Revisit the list as often as you feel there is a need to.

Doing so will identify the words that are most meaningful to you at that particular time.

They are a true expression of where you are on your grief journey.

Freely change, delete or add words.

Abandoned

Absentminded

Abused

Acceptance

Acknowledgement

Adjusted

Afraid

Aged

Agitated

Aimless

Alive

Alone

Ambivalent

Anger

Anguish

Annoyed

Anxious

Apathetic

Appalled

Arrogant

Avoidance

Betrayed

Bewildered

Bitter

Blameful

Blindsided

Bombarded

Bothered

Broken

Cautious

Chaos

Cheated

Choice

Closure

Comfort

Conflict

Confrontational

Confused

Controlled

Courageous

Cowardly

Crazy

Cross

Crushed

Dead

Deceived

Denial

Depleted

Depressed

Desire

Despair

Devastated

Diminished

Disappointed

Disbelief

Disconnected

Discontent

Discouraged

Disloyal

Dismayed

Disorganized

Disoriented

Distracted

Distress

Drained

Dread

Empathy

Envy

Exasperated

Exhausted

Expectations

Exploited

Explosive

Failure

Fear

Finality

Forgetful

Forgiveness

Free

Frustration

Fulfilled

Furious

Guilt

Happy

Harassed

Hate

Healing

Heartache

Helpless

Hesitant

Hollow

Hope

Hopeful

Hopeless

Horror

Hostile

Humble

Humor

Hurt

Hypersensitive

Hysterical

Idealization

Identity

Ignored

Impaired

Impatient

Incensed

Incomplete

Indifferent

Indignant

Indulgent

Insecure

Insulted

Intolerant

Irritated

Irrational

Isolated

Jealous

Joy

Judged

Kindness

Laughter

Lifeless

Listless

Logical

Lonely

Longing

Loss

Lost

Love

Mad

Mean

Meditative

Memorialize

Miserable

Misunderstood

Moody

Negative

Nervous

Numb

Obstinate

Offended

Optimistic

Out of control

Outraged

Overbearing

Overcome

Overprotective

Overwhelmed

Pain

Panic

Patience

Peace

Perplexed

Perturbed

Pining

Powerless

Pressure

Provoked

Puzzled

Quiet

Rage

Rant

Rave

Realization

Recovery

Reflection

Regret

Reinvestment

Rejected

Relaxed

Relief

Reorganized

Repressed

Resentment

Resilient

Restless

Ridiculed

Robbed

Sad

Scared

Scarred

Scattered

Searching

Self-doubt

Selfish

Sensitive

Serene

Shame

Shock

Silent

Smothered

Sobbing

Spiritual

Startled

Stress

Stoic

Sulky

Supported

Surprised

Surreal

Survivorship

Suspicious

Sympathetic

Talkative

Tearful

Tense

Ticked off

Threatened

Tolerant

Tormented

Torn

Transformed

Undecided

Understood

Unfocused

Unreal

Unsupported

Uptight

Validated

Victimized

Vindictive

Violated

Volatile

Vulnerable

Weepy

Withdrawn

Worried

Yearning

WHAT HELPS THE MOST?

Lives are redefined by the death of a child and it takes however long it needs to take to discover a "New Normal" life.

Your grief needs and feelings are ever changing as you grow and heal on your grief journey.

The key to this transformation is you.
You can survive if you choose to do so.
You can have a meaningful life again.
You can't change what has happened however you can change how you react.
Search for a sense of purpose and meaning will return.

Give yourself permission and time to experience emotions associated with your loss.
There is no timeline on this journey.
Time can heal depending on what you do with it.

Learn the skills and tools necessary, which teach you how to cope, ease your pain, survive, find hope for healing and reinvest in living life again.

Educate yourself, meet other bereaved families, share, tell and retell your story, read books, attend support groups, bereavement programs, workshops or conferences. It may be helpful to use a highlighter for books or articles you read or take notes on index cards or in a journal/notebook.

This is not a short-term process or long-term process, but rather a lifetime process.

Grieve for the loss of what was, what is and for the future you don't get to create.

Be patient with yourself and grieve at your own pace.
Take some time out of your day to take care of you. Even if it is just fifteen minutes a day, make that commitment to yourself.

Hold onto hope it is your life preserver and beacon of light in the darkness.

Create/Develop a strong network of support: Attend support group meetings (The Compassionate Friends, Bereaved Parents of the USA, Hospices etc.) conferences or private counseling.

Check out resources or other outreach programs that are available.

Tell and retell your story.

Surround yourself with people who will listen, understand and support you. Do not be surprised that your "address book changes".

Working your grief requires both listening and being heard.

It is just as important to be heard, as it is to listen.

Shared grief is diminished grief.

Give people permission to say your child's name.

Cry when you need to for as long as you need to and always have tissues on hand.

Tears are healthy, cleansing, exhausting and not a sign of weakness.

Nourish and replenish your body. You may have to force yourself to do this.

Eat small amounts of healthy nutritious foods frequently.

Do not binge eat (comfort food).

Keep hydrated drink plenty of fluids; moisturize your skin, hair and lips. Keep water, moisturizing lotion, Chap Stick or lip balm, and hard candy or gum on hand.

Get plenty of rest.

Exercise, take a five-minute walk, stretch, do some yoga or get a massage.

Be flexible, fluctuations will occur, expect the unexpected, have a plan A & B for back up.

Avoid triggers (place, sight, sound, smell, taste, memory, tradition) or situations that arouse grief.

Triggers will always be there – often they help you move through the healing process.

They may come from self-blame, frustration, mood, sleep disturbances, resentment, revenge, hurt, fear, helplessness, hopelessness and failure to receive desired support from family and friends.

Always have a pen, pad and date book on hand and on your nightstand, have duplicate sets of car, home and work keys, have an automobile roadside assistance membership, a centrally located calendar and use a timer when cooking inside or barbequing outside.

Set attainable goals.

Encourage communication, openness and exploration of feelings.

Consider the entire family when making plans.
Ask for help.

Let family friends and coworkers help with practical daily things such as grocery shopping, local trips to the bank, cleaners, post office or pharmacy, doing a load of laundry, setting the table, cooking a meal or picking up one, do the dishes or load the dishwasher, take out the garbage, yard work, take your car to a car wash or for servicing.

Preserve keepsakes, pictures, video, audio recordings etc., make copies, laminate pictures, drawings, documents, store in airtight/waterproof/fireproof container. If these things disturb you, put them away for now. If they comfort you keep them accessible.

Relieve your stress.

Scream, cry, laugh, and write a letter to your child, journal or take up a new hobby. Some examples are arts and crafts, puzzles, gardening, cooking, baking, knitting, crocheting, quilting, movement or pet therapy, dance, imagery, acupuncture, meditation, yoga, aromatherapy, massage, long baths, exercise, sports (bowling, golfing, tennis, swimming, cycling, kick boxing, learn karate, white water rafting, scuba diving, bird watching, hunting, boating, fishing) travel, poetry, listen to music,

play an instrument, go to the movies, take a vacation, volunteer or learn photography.
Spend more time getting in touch with nature; take a stroll on the beach or a walk in the park.

Go to different stores than you did with your child.
Shop by catalog or online.

Visit the cemetery when it is less crowded.
Memorialize your child, attend candle lighting ceremonies, balloon or butterfly releases, tree of memory dedications, walks to remember, plant a garden, form a scholarship fund, make donations to charities of your choice etc.
Keep your child remembered. Pictures can be used for stamps, address labels, ornaments, snow globes, mouse pads, mugs, throw blankets etc.

Remember the love, celebrate the life and share the journey.

TAKING BETTER CARE OF YOU

Directions: Read over the list and check any which would enable you to take better care of yourself. Freely add what you don't see.

___ Take more time to be with family
___ Leave work at work
___ Call a friend
___ Write a letter
___ Journal
___ Listen to music
___ Buy some new music
___ Sing
___ Play an instrument
___ Get more physical exercise
___ Walk, jog, run
___ Cycling
___ Gym, work out, aerobics
___ Dance
___ Yoga, Meditation, Imagery
___ Movement, aroma or pet therapy
___ Swim
___ Tennis
___ Golf
___ Baseball, softball
___ Bowl
___ Basketball
___ Hockey
___ Football
___ Scuba dive
___ Enjoy more leisure time
___ Sleep more or less/take a nap

____ Leave weekend's open
____ Travel
____ See friends more often
____ Make new friends
____ Go to the theatre, concert, movies
____ Dance
____ Enjoy more leisure reading
____ Get more humor in your life
____ Clean out your closets
____ Buy some new clothes
____ Treat yourself to something you've wanted
____ Start and finish household projects
____ Take a class
____ Go on a retreat
____ Enjoy more outdoor activities
____ Express your talent
____ Doing art
____ Creative
____ Cooking
____ Gardening
____ Other _____

____ Improve your diet
____ Eat small frequent amounts of healthy
        nutritious food
____ Less fast food
____ Less junk food
____ Less salt, fatty foods, caffeine, red meats
____ Eat more fruits, grains and vegetables
____ Other _____

DO'S AND DON'TS
WHEN HELPING A NEWLY
BEREAVED PARENT

Many people feel helpless to make a difference when facing the death of a child.
They often express their frustration about not knowing how to help, what to do or say, or how to "fix it."

Bereaved parents are more likely to have a nurturing grief journey if they have hope and a continuous network of positive support and understanding.

Bereaved parents don't know how to go on living without their child and can't imagine their world without their child in it.

Bereaved parents trying to endure the incomprehensible are bombarded with a myriad of unanswered questions, overwhelming changes emotionally, physically, behaviorally and spiritually.

The following suggested do's and don'ts are for those accompanying you on your grief journey.

Do walk beside us and be there for us.
We need your unconditional love.

Do be empathetic and patient with us.
Show love and concern.
Write us a condolence letter.
Ask if, we'd mind talking about what happened
or if it would be too painful?
Talk about your own losses and share how you
coped.

Do be present.
Help with practical things, household chores,
vacuuming, loading, unloading the dishwasher,
change sheets on the bed, grocery shop, cook
a meal or pick up one, go to the cleaners, the
bank, post office, do car pools to pick up the
kids, baby-sit, offer to shop for special occasion
or holiday gifts that we are not up to shopping
for, take out the garbage, water plants or mow
the lawn, drive family members to
appointments or support groups, make a cup of
coffee and sit awhile. Encourage us to talk
about our child.
During the wake, take calls; make airport runs,
stock up with food, paper goods, coffee, cake,
tissues and toilet paper.

Make a list of any masses being offered in
memory of our child or address and stamp
sympathy envelopes for us.

Attend to surviving siblings' a.k.a. the forgotten mourners and acknowledge their loss.
Bereaved siblings need to have their grief acknowledged even by their grieving parents.

Do give yourself permission to talk to surviving siblings and us about our child/sibling.
You'll cause more pain by not mentioning our child/sibling.
Sharing memories and laughter helps our hearts heal.
We grieve by remembering not forgetting.
Telling and retelling our story helps our child to be remembered. Asking questions and telling us stories we may or may not know is priceless.

Do be a sounding board a.k.a. loving listener.
Listening can be more effective than you know.
Let bereaved parents experience and express their disbelief, pain, despair and questions.
Repetition is part of the healing process.

Do honor our child's life.
Acknowledge that our child did exist by contacting us on their birthday, death date, holidays and special occasions or by sending us cards, thoughtful notes, an email, text message or calling on these days when we miss them so.

Encourage new traditions (Birthdays, Anniversaries, Holidays, Special Occasions).
Donate to a favorite charity in our child's memory. Be sure that they notify us.
Contribute to our foundation or scholarship fund.
Have a tree planted in our child's memory or star named after our child.
Attend Candle Lighting remembrance, Balloon or Butterfly release ceremonies with us.
Donate a book to a support group in our child's memory.
Make a memory jar, box, book or album for us.

Do encourage us to get out of bed, go for a walk, keep a journal, go to a movie, shop or read a book about handling our grief.

Do remind us to eat healthy, drink plenty of fluids, get rest and exercise, keep appointments and pay our bills. We need this!

Do let us know that smiles can return and that life will be tolerable again.
Remind us to set realistic goals
Let us grieve at our own pace.

Don't call or say, "If there is anything I can do let me know."
We have no idea what we need.

Just do it. For example: I shop on Tuesday (it's Monday) what items can I pick up for you. When we need the help most we are not able to ask for it.

Don't expect us to reach out and pick up the phone when we are so overwhelmed, exhausted and don't even know what we need.

Don't offer clichés.
There are no words to rid us of pain.
Sometimes what needs to be said can be said non-verbally; your presence, hug or touch of a hand can replace the need for words in shared silence. It's okay if you cry! It helps us too!
If you don't know what to say then say nothing or simply say that you are sorry or that you cannot find the right words to bring comfort.
Sometimes well-intended words can be hurtful rather than consoling.

Don't try to eliminate, fix our grief or offer solutions.
You can't fix this.
You can't take our grief away from us or grieve for us.

Don't try to make our tears go away.
Let us cry when we must for as long as we need to.

Uncontrollable floodgates of tears a.k.a. grief
burst or melt down moments arrive unsolicited,
wherever and whenever they want.
Tears are an expression of what we are feeling,
a release of emotions are not a sign of
weakness.
Crying can be a shared experience in
acknowledging the death of a loved one.
Crying is healthy.

Don't pass judgment with "you should."
Do not "should" on me or on yourself.

Don't tell us what to do with our child's
possessions.
Give us time to sort things out when we are
ready.
Each of us has our own time schedule when to
let things go.
You might ask us our plans to get us thinking.
Encourage us to make careful non-impulsive
decisions. We can be impulsive at this time.
Our child's room may become a shrine.
Our child's personal belongings are a link to
our child and are treasured keepsakes.
Some of us find comfort in preserving
memories and leaving everything as it was.
Others find peace in their child's room by lying
across their bed, wrapping ourselves up in their
blanket, smelling their pillow or clothes,
wearing jewelry or an article of their clothing.

Some of us pack up their belongings until we decide what to do with them.
Some of us gift cherished items to dear friends and relatives as a way to remember our child.
Some of us donate belongings to charitable groups. Take your time with this one!

Don't remove pictures of our child from your home and erase them as if they didn't exist.
By displaying pictures and mementos of our child you keep them remembered. None of us want our child erased.

Don't tell us how we should react.
Bereaved parents often become hypersensitive to their surroundings and moods can fluctuate on a roller coaster of feelings and emotions.
We may even be angry – that's part of the grief process.
We have a right to do things differently, to change our minds if we want to and to also have "alone" time.

Don't be afraid of us or avoid us as if we are part of some secret society or have a plague/disease.
The death of our child is not contagious!
Say hello instead of crossing the street or seeking a different aisle in the grocery store to avoid us.

The death of a child makes people uncomfortable. We know this! Be brave! Often people don't know how to react or relate to us and get tired of being around someone who is sad.
Not everyone who was there before our child's death will be there afterwards.
Family and friend relationships change, as does our address book.

Don't give up on us if we decline invitations. We may be unable to attend family functions, holiday or special occasions because we need time to adapt to the situation. Give us time to become social again when we are ready, not when you think we should be ready. Please keep asking not pushing.

Don't call us to complain about your spouse, the kids, your job, car trouble or a broken nail. The death of our child has been life altering, our priorities change and what once was important now seems insignificant.

Don't invalidate our grief by making insensitive remarks.

Don't try to one up us or tell us you know how I feel because your dog just died. You don't know how I feel.

Don't say, "How are you handling it?"
We take it one breath, second, minute, hour,
day or step at a time.
How about how's today going for you?

Don't say, "I don't know how you do it."
It's not like we have a choice. The death of our
child goes on forever.

Don't say, "Aren't you over it yet?" or "When
are you going to get over it or find closure?"
We never find closure or get over the death of
our child.
We learn to accept what we cannot change and
to live with it and through it.
It doesn't just go away or have a time schedule.
It takes as long as it needs to take.

Don't say, "Everything happens for a reason"
or "It's God's will."
The death of a child is not reasonable.
The death of a child challenges one's religious
and spiritual beliefs.
We aren't supposed to bury our child.
We continue to ask questions until we wear
them out.
Why would God do this to us?
Why now?
Why not me instead of my child?
Why?

Don't say, "Get on with your life" or "It's time to move on."
What life?
How?
Our mind is numb and we can't think straight.
Our lives are shattered, consumed by grief with a relentless unending hollow empty void that aches and yearns for our child.
We have all we can do to get out of bed.
We barely function on the fumes of autopilot in a fog-like state while trying to grasp how life and the world continue to go on all around us when our child has died.
It's too much to endure and we can't comprehend facing a future without our child in it.
We wonder how long or if we well ever genuinely smile, laugh or experience joy in our lives again.
There is no timetable on this journey.
Grief work cannot be done on a fixed schedule.
There are no short cuts, magic wands, pills, words or slogans that can reverse what has happened.
No one can take our grief from us or do it for us.
It is our journey.

Don't ask, "Are you feeling better?"
We're not sick and this is not an illness, we are grieving and mourning the death of our child.

Don't say, "You're so strong" or "You are doing so well."
We're not strong, just numb and going through the motions of daily living like a robot.

Don't say, "Be thankful for your other children", "At least you are young enough to have another child" or "You can always adopt."
Our children are not interchangeable.
Our child is dead and not replaceable.

Don't say, "They are in a much better place."
Not when I want to hug and hold them right here.

Don't say, "It's good that your child died quickly" or "At least they aren't suffering."
There is no good way for a child to die.

Don't say, "Your child wouldn't want you to be sad."
We know that.

Don't say, "Time heals" or "Keep your chin up."
Time can and does heal depending on what we do with time.

DEALING WITH A BEREAVED SIBLING

By Laura Ameruso

A sibling is part of your past, present and future. Almost your entire life is spent with your sibling, whether you are the older taking on the parent role or younger looking up to your sibling, a best friend. They are part of your identity.

Society sometimes fails to validate sibling grief, we deal with disenfranchised grief as sympathy goes to the parents and siblings are suppose to "get over it" and take care of parents. You never get over it, you learn how to get through it.

As a bereaved sibling I provide insight to parents on dealing with your bereaved children whose brother or sister passed away. My brother Jason Lee and father Anthony passed within three months of each other and my life was forever changed. Our family tree is broken, family dynamics and structure has changed. Each new day brings a new challenge during this grief journey.

Siblings have a special bond since birth, our childhood and reaching adulthood and the belief we will bury our parents. It's not supposed to be this way. We are supposed to grow old together, our children, and reminisce about our family.

We feel now we must care for our parents which causes us to forget our pain, forget that we also need to grieve. This chronic pain of losing a sibling seems to suffocate you at times. A bereaved parent cannot give us the security we need as children. They are hurting themselves.

Through your grief a parent needs to find a way to communicate with your other children. Find time, share moments and special memories to validate your relationship. Talk about them, talk to your child, tell the story of their birth, funny stories that we, as siblings were too young to remember.

As a sibling I share stories with my Mom. She has learned more about Jason and I gave her new memories to now hold in her heart. This brings us closer and makes those tough days a little easier. Of course I have secrets only a brother and sister shares.

Although we are grieving for the same person in our lives, we grieve differently. We share similar feelings at times as you have learned throughout this book about dealing with grief we feel we are going crazy at times too. Depending on our age within the family, that determines the beginning of our grief journey.

As we learn to move forward during our grief, we will never let go of our cherished memories. It takes courage to understand this change and have the strength to keep moving forward.

Factors associated with bereaved siblings:

Age

Family Structure

Younger or older sibling – birth order

Roles within the family – older/younger sibling

Meaning of the death

Circumstances surrounding the death

Trauma/ witness to suffering

Guilt if we were not there at passing

Last relationship/friendships

Loss of a future

Question of our own mortality

Life space – shared friends, leisure time, school

CLOSING THOUGHTS

The path to healing is through your pain.
It requires your active participation that is
essential for healing.

If you don't give yourself permission to mourn
and grieve you will stay frozen in pain,
immobilized and your life will have stopped
where your loss left you.

May you find comfort in knowing that the
intensity of your pain and suffering will not last
forever, it becomes tolerable.

While you cannot go back to who you were
before this catastrophic event, you can live fully
as who you are now and who you are includes
what you did for and with your child.

Your child's death will be with you forever,
however so will your child's life.
You are the keeper of the memories.

You can not only survive your loss but also
heal and grow because of it.

It is my hope that by validating and confirming
what you are feeling or have felt that you will
realize that you are not alone on this journey.

Death ends a life, but certainly not the
relationship or love shared.

You are not going crazy.

I AM

I Am

Crying behind this mask of mourning
Tears hidden beneath its disguise
Invisible to the world around me
There are no answers to the question why
So I have stopped asking

I let you go
I let you fly
You pad the price
With your life

No longer estranged are we
For in your death
Forgiveness has set us free
We share a bond you and I
As only a mother and son could have
Forever that will be so

My tears are for the remnants of
Tomorrows shattered dreams
I mourn for the loss of
What might or could have been
Life has such a different meaning now

Never will you be forgotten
By the lives you touched
The warmth of your love is captured
Forever in our hearts
Cherished and embraced in
Tomorrows summer shade and
Winter's necklaces

Until we meet again my son
May you soar the Heavens
On angels' wings
I love you so very much

Written by Mark Anthony's Mom,
Diana M. Cimador Roscigno

THE RENAISSANCE MAN

The Renaissance Man

What Are Human Gifts?

I think I can safely say and think at this very moment that most of us do not dwell on the topic too often. God provides messengers in this area in unique ways sometimes softly and sometimes with extreme intensity – even most tragically.

We all have these beautiful gifts in varying degrees, but we do recognize that Godly reality. The Renaissance was an explosion of thoughts, deeds and accomplishments. The Sistine Chapel is the epitome of mans wondrous ability to think, do and accomplish. One would argue that nothing is impossible – even landing on the moon.

It has been my experience in life that those born with a preponderance of Godly gifts are most humble about the situation – they just do, no matter what the challenge.

When I think of Mark, I think of these human gifts, He was extremely bright, extremely dedicated to task be it academic, physical sport, scouting, music, love of nature, plus his complete tenacity of deed to such – again, in a most unassuming manner.

Yes, I always refer to Mark as a Renaissance man. He truly is and will always be that to me.

Written in memory of my grandson,
Mark Anthony Governale
By Fausto R. Cimador

GRIEF RESOURCES

Alive Alone
1112 Champaign Dr.
Van Wert, Ohio 45891
EM: alivalon@bright.net
Support for bereaved parents whose only child or all children are deceased

American Association of Suicidology
2459 South Ash St.
Denver, Colorado 80222
(303) 692-0985
www.suicidology.org
Supplies literature and referrals to survivors of suicide

Bereaved Parents of the USA
National Headquarters
PO Box 95
Park Forest, Illinois 60466
(708) 748-7866
www.bereavedparentsusa.org
Bereaved Parents of the USA (BP/USA) is a national organization, offering self-help support groups for bereaved parents and their families who are struggling to survive after the death of a child

Centering Corporation
PO Box 4600
Omaha, Nebraska 68104
(402) 523- 1200 or 1-(866) 218-0101
www.centering.org or www.griefdigest.com
Grief Resource Center, support, information and hope

Comfort Zone Camp, Inc.
80 Park St.
Montclair, New Jersey 07042
1-(866) 4848-5679 or 1-(973) 364-1717
www.comfortzonecamp.org
Comfort Zone Camp is the nation's largest camp program for children 7 years old to 12th. grade, who have experienced the death of a parent, sibling or primary caretaker – for free!

The Compassionate Friends
PO Box 3696
Oak Brook, Illinois 60522-3696
1-(877) 969-0010
www.compassionatefriends.org
Information and resources for families who have experienced the death of a child

Concerns of Police Survivors (COPS)
PO Box 3199, S. Highway 5
Camdenton, Missouri 65020
1-(573) 346-4911
www.nationalcops.org
Support for law enforcement officers and their families who have been affected by death and bereavement

Grief Recovery After Substance Passing (GRASP)
Denise & Gary Cullen
42-335 Washington St. Ste.#175
Palm Desert, CA 92211
1-760-262-8612 or 714-865-7879
www.grasphelp.org
Support, information and resources for families who have had a loved one die through drugs

Mothers Against Drunk Driving (MADD)
511 E. John Carpenter Freeway, Suite 700
Irving, Texas 75062-8187
1-(800)-GET-MADD
www.maddorg
Education, resources and advocacy for bereaved families

National SIDS/Infant Death Resource Center
8280 Greensboro Dr., Suite 300
McLean, Virginia 22102
1-(866) 866-7437
Resources for information about sudden infant death syndrome and support for those affected by SIDS

Parents of Murdered Children (POMC)
100 E. 8th. St., Suite B-41
Cincinnati, Ohio 45202
1-(888)-818-POMC
www.pomc.com
Support for survivors of homicide

Tragedy Assistance Program for Survivors (TAPS)
2001 S. Street NW, Suite 300
Washington, DC 20009
1-(800) 959-8277
www.taps.org
Support and assistance for members of the armed services who experience death and bereavement

NOTES

NOTES